LE CORDON BLEU

HOME COLLECTION

·ITALIAN·

MURDOCH BOOKS®

Sydney • London • Vancouver • New York

contents

4
Minestrone

6
Artichoke, spinach and pine nut salad

8
Garlic and zucchini soup

10
Fritto misto with a garlic dip

12
*Crostini with tapenade/Prosciutto,
smoked ham and mustard roulade*

14
Roman gnocchi

16
Parmesan tulips with eggplant caviar

18
*Bruschetta with Parma ham,
Gorgonzola and sun-dried tomatoes*

20
Tomato and balsamic vinegar salad

22
Grilled scallops with prosciutto

24
Mushroom ravioli in rosemary garlic cream

26
Seafood risotto

28
Tagliatelle with wild mushrooms and leeks

30
Veal parmigiana

32
Cannelloni with spinach

34
Osso buco

36
Pasta with prosciutto and Parmesan

38
Veal with lemon and capers

40
Venetian-style liver

42
*Rabbit and marjoram cobbler
with herb scones*

44
Classic lasagne

46
Chicken cacciatore

48
Mediterranean vegetables with polenta cakes

50
Sicilian cheesecake

52
Zuccotto

54
Tiramisù

56
*Baked peaches with
mascarpone cream*

58
Chocolate hazelnut torte

60
Zabaglione with sponge fingers

62
Chef's techniques

recipe ratings ✸ *easy* ✸✸ *a little more care needed* ✸✸✸ *more care needed*

Minestrone

Although there are many variations of this hearty soup, according to the region it comes from and the season, it will always consist of vegetables and broth with the addition of pasta or rice.

Preparation time 45 minutes + overnight soaking
Total cooking time 2 hours 20 minutes
Serves 6–8

250 g (8 oz) dried beans, such as kidney beans or navy beans
150 g (5 oz) diced salt pork or belly bacon
2 tablespoons olive oil
1 large onion, chopped
2 carrots, diced
2 potatoes, diced
1 celery stick, diced
2 cloves garlic, chopped
1 tablespoon tomato paste
3 litres beef stock or water
bouquet garni
1/4 cabbage, finely sliced
150 g (5 oz) dried macaroni or any small pasta
grated Parmesan, to serve

1 Cover the beans with cold water and leave to soak for 8 hours or overnight. Drain, place in a large pan with 2 litres water and simmer for 1 1/2 hours, or until tender.
2 Meanwhile, place the salt pork or bacon in another pan and cover with cold water. Bring to the boil, strain and refresh in cold water. Spread on paper towels to dry. In a large heavy-based pan, heat the olive oil and lightly brown the salt pork or bacon over medium heat for 3 minutes. Add the onion, carrot, potato, celery and garlic, reduce the heat and cook for 5 minutes without colouring. Add the tomato paste and cook for 3 minutes. Add the stock and simmer for 10 minutes, skimming any fat from the surface. Add the bouquet garni and cabbage and simmer for 5 minutes. Remove from the heat and set aside.
3 Drain the beans and add to the soup mixture. Return to the heat and simmer for 10 minutes. Add the pasta and cook for another 15 minutes, or until soft. Check the seasoning and remove the bouquet garni. Serve with the grated Parmesan sprinkled over the top.

Artichoke, spinach and pine nut salad

*This fresh-tasting salad could either be served as a first course,
or with crusty bread as a light lunch on a hot summer's day.*

*Preparation time **40 minutes***
*Total cooking time **30 minutes***
Serves 4

4 large fresh artichokes
juice of 2 lemons
150 g (5 oz) baby English spinach leaves
80 g (2³/4 oz) pine nuts, toasted
2 tablespoons olive oil
40 g (1¹/4 oz) grated Parmesan
16 black olives, halved and pitted

1 Prepare the fresh artichokes, following the method in the Chef's techniques on page 63. When you place the artichokes in the pan of boiling water, use the juice from one of the lemons in the water. Once you have cooked and prepared the artichokes, cut them into bite-size wedges, cover and set aside.

2 In a large bowl toss the spinach leaves with the pine nuts. Whisk the olive oil with 1 tablespoon lemon juice and freshly ground black pepper, to taste, and use to dress the spinach. Divide the artichoke pieces among four bowls and pile the spinach up in the centre. Top the salad with the Parmesan and black olives.

Garlic and zucchini soup

Two whole bulbs of garlic may seem a powerfully large amount, but you will find it takes on a mellow creaminess when cooked.

Preparation time **35 minutes**
Total cooking time **1 hour 15 minutes**
Serves 4–6

olive oil, for cooking
1 onion, finely chopped
2 bulbs garlic, peeled and thinly sliced
2 potatoes, peeled and thinly sliced
2 litres chicken stock or water
2 zucchini (courgettes)
1 tablespoon finely chopped fresh basil

1 Heat about 4 tablespoons of olive oil in a large heavy-based pan, add the onion and garlic and cook over medium heat for 5–10 minutes, or until golden brown. Add the potato and cook for 2 minutes, stirring continuously. Add the stock, season to taste with salt and pepper and then simmer for 30 minutes. Allow to cool a little.

2 Trim the ends from the zucchini. Cut into quarters lengthways, then cut into short pieces. Set aside.

3 Purée the soup in a blender or food processor until smooth. Return to the pan and bring to the boil. Skim any foam from the top if necessary, then add the zucchini and cook for 20–25 minutes, or until the zucchini is tender. Just before serving, stir in the basil and adjust the seasoning. Serve garnished with a few extra basil leaves.

Fritto misto with a garlic dip

There are a number of ways to prepare Italy's well-known mixed fry. Here the fish is simply dipped in flour, egg and then breadcrumbs before being fried to a crispy golden brown.

Preparation time **1 hour**
Total cooking time **20 minutes**
Serves 6 as a starter or 2 as a main course.

2 French shallots, finely chopped
150 ml (5 fl oz) dry white wine
1 bay leaf
1 sprig of fresh thyme
300 g (10 oz) mussels, scrubbed and beards removed
150 g (5 oz) squid
oil, for deep-frying
4 eggs, lightly beaten
90 g (3 oz) plain flour, seasoned with salt and pepper
200 g (6¹/² oz) fresh breadcrumbs
150 g (5 oz) barramundi, plaice, sole or flounder fillet, cut into strips
150 g (5 oz) blue-eye cod, ling or cod fillet, cut into large, bite-size cubes
185 g (6 oz) mayonnaise
1 tablespoon plain yoghurt
2 cloves garlic, finely chopped
fresh parsley and lemon wedges, to garnish

1 Put the shallot, wine, bay leaf and thyme in a large saucepan, cover and bring to the boil. Add the mussels, discarding any that are already open, cover and reduce to medium heat. Cook for 2 minutes, shaking the pan occasionally, until the mussels open (discard any that do not open). Drain and remove from the shells.

2 To prepare the squid, remove the wings from the tube, peel off the skin and remove the head. Remove the clear cartilage quill from the opening of the tube, cut off the tentacles and rinse the tube under running water. Drain, dry, then slice into rings.

3 One-third fill a large heavy-based pan with oil and heat to 190°C (375°F). Put the egg, flour and breadcrumbs into separate dishes. Toss the fish, mussels and squid in the flour, shake off the excess, then dip into the egg and finally coat with the breadcrumbs, shaking off the excess. Deep-fry the crumbed seafood in batches until golden brown, drain on crumpled paper towels and sprinkle lightly with salt. If keeping warm for a few minutes, do so on a wire rack in a warm oven, uncovered.

4 To make the garlic dip, stir together the mayonnaise, yoghurt and garlic and serve in a bowl to accompany the seafood. Garnish with the parsley and lemon wedges.

Crostini with tapenade

Crostini are Italian croutes, ideal with soups or as an accompaniment to vegetable dishes and salads. Here they are served with a tapenade, which is very intense in flavour and should be spread thinly.

Preparation time **15 minutes**
Total cooking time **25 minutes**
Makes about 60

I French baguette
olive oil, for cooking
60 g (2 oz) black olives, pitted
I small clove garlic
8 anchovy fillets

1 Preheat the oven to moderate 180°C (350°F/Gas 4). Cut the bread into very thin slices. Pour enough of the oil into a large frying pan to lightly coat the base and heat gently. Lightly fry the bread, in batches, on both sides, then transfer to a baking tray. Bake in the oven until both sides are golden. Remove and cool to room temperature.

2 To make the tapenade, place the olives, garlic and anchovy fillets in a food processor and work into a paste with a spreadable consistency, adding a little olive oil if it is too dry. Season with freshly ground black pepper, but avoid salt—the saltiness of the anchovies will be enough. Spread sparingly over the crostini.

Prosciutto, smoked ham and mustard roulade

Simple to prepare, yet full of flavour, these are ideal for serving with cocktails or pre-dinner drinks.

Preparation time **15 minutes + 10 minutes chilling**
Total cooking time **5 minutes**
Makes about 35

100 g (3¹/4 oz) smoked ham trimmings
60 g (2 oz) mayonnaise
I tablespoon Dijon mustard
100 g (3¹/4 oz) prosciutto slices
3 stale petits pains (small French rolls)
fresh chervil, to garnish

1 To make the filling, purée the ham trimmings in a food processor, add the mayonnaise and mustard and process to bind. Season with salt and freshly ground black pepper.

2 Lay the slices of prosciutto, slightly overlapping, on a sheet of plastic wrap and spread the filling mixture over the prosciutto with the back of a spoon. Roll up the prosciutto lengthways and put in the freezer for 10 minutes to firm.

3 Thinly slice the petits pains and toast until golden brown. Cut the prosciutto roll into thin slices and place a slice on each piece of toasted bread. Garnish with the fresh chervil.

Crostini with tapenade (top)
and Prosciutto, smoked ham and mustard roulade

Roman gnocchi

The extremely popular Italian gnocchi can be made from potato, pumpkin or, as in this case, semolina. Often served as a starter, gnocchi are also perfect for lunch, accompanied by a crisp green salad.

Preparation time **35 minutes + 30 minutes cooling**
Total cooking time **2 hours 20 minutes**
Serves 4 as a starter

40 g (1 1/4 oz) unsalted butter
60 g (2 oz) bacon, diced
1 small onion, chopped
1 small carrot, chopped
2 tablespoons tomato paste
1 tablespoon plain flour
500 g (1 lb) tomatoes, peeled, seeded and chopped
bouquet garni
4 cloves garlic, chopped
500 ml (16 fl oz) chicken stock or water

GNOCCHI
500 ml (16 fl oz) milk
60 g (2 oz) unsalted butter
150 g (5 oz) semolina flour or fine semolina
30 g (1 oz) plain flour
2 tablespoons thick (double) cream
1 egg
2 egg yolks
4 tablespoons freshly grated Parmesan
80 g (2 3/4 oz) unsalted butter, melted

1 Preheat the oven to moderate 180°C (350°F/Gas 4). Melt the butter in a flameproof dish and cook the bacon until golden brown. Add the onion and carrot and cook for 3 minutes. Stir in the tomato paste and cook for 2 minutes. Sprinkle with the flour, place in the oven for 5 minutes, then stir until the flour disappears. Add the tomato, bouquet garni and garlic, return to the stove top and cook for 5 minutes, stirring. Stir in the stock and boil for 2 minutes. Cover and cook in the oven for 1 hour. Strain into a clean pan and discard the solids. Bring the sauce back to the boil on the stove top and skim if necessary. Lower the heat and simmer for 20 minutes, or until thickened. Season, to taste, with salt and black pepper, set aside and keep warm.

2 To make the gnocchi, bring the milk and butter to the boil in a large pan. Add the flours and stir over low heat until absorbed, then stir for 5 minutes longer, or until the mixture rolls off the side of the pan. Remove from the heat, add the cream, egg, egg yolks and half the Parmesan and stir until smooth. Season, to taste, and spread 1 cm (1/2 inch) thick on a baking tray lined with baking paper. Cool for 30 minutes, then cut into rounds with a wet 4 cm (1 1/2 inch) cutter. Put in an ovenproof dish, drizzle with the melted butter and sprinkle with the remaining Parmesan. Bake for 20 minutes, or until golden, and serve with the tomato sauce.

Parmesan tulips with eggplant caviar

Although rather time consuming to prepare, the beautiful presentation of this dish, combining colours and complementary flavours, will make an impressive start to any meal.

Preparation time 25 minutes + 30 minutes marinating
  + 1 hour refrigeration
Total cooking time 1 hour
Makes 10

4 red capsicums (peppers)
1 teaspoon lemon juice
4 tablespoons olive oil
150 g (5 oz) Parmesan, grated

EGGPLANT (AUBERGINE) CAVIAR
800 g (1 lb 10 oz) eggplant (aubergine)
60 ml (2 fl oz) olive oil
50 g (1³/4 oz) black olives, pitted and chopped
1 clove garlic, crushed
10 g (¹/4 oz) fresh chives, finely chopped
¹/2 teaspoon paprika

1 Halve the capsicums, removing the seeds and membrane. Place in a dish and sprinkle with salt and freshly ground black pepper. Stir the lemon juice into the olive oil, pour over the capsicums, cover and marinate for at least 30 minutes and up to 2 hours. Preheat the oven to moderate 180°C (350°F/Gas 4).
2 To make the eggplant caviar, cut the eggplants in half lengthways. Brush the cut side with a little of the olive oil and sprinkle with salt and pepper. Place on an oven tray and bake for 25 minutes, or until soft. Drain to remove the liquid and scrape out the flesh with a spoon. Roughly chop the flesh and combine with the olives, garlic and chives, reserving some chives for the garnish. Mix well with a fork, squeezing the eggplant against the side of the bowl to break it down. Add the remaining olive oil very slowly, stirring it in with the fork. Add the paprika and season to taste. Refrigerate for 1 hour.
3 To make the Parmesan tulips, draw two 10 cm (4 inch) circles on a sheet of baking paper and place on a baking tray. Sprinkle a thick layer of Parmesan in each circle. Bake in the oven for 3–5 minutes, or until bubbled with lightly golden-brown edges. Cool for a few moments, then lift off with a palette knife or spatula. Shape into tulips by moulding over the top of a bottle neck, pleating the edges and holding in place until cooled. Repeat with the remaining Parmesan.
4 Preheat a chargrill pan, barbecue or grill, brush with oil and cook the capsicums for 5 minutes each side, or until tender. Remove the skin and cut the capsicums into strips. Place a heaped tablespoon of eggplant caviar in each Parmesan tulip and sprinkle with the reserved chives. Arrange the capsicum in crosses around the tulips and serve.

Bruschetta with Parma ham, Gorgonzola and sun-dried tomatoes

Italians are great bread-eaters. Bruschetta are thin slices of bread, grilled and rubbed with a clove of cut garlic—the original garlic bread.

Preparation time **10 minutes**
Total cooking time **5 minutes**
Makes 8

1 loaf Italian country bread
2 cloves garlic, halved
60 ml (2 fl oz) extra virgin olive oil
8 pieces sun-dried tomato in olive oil
200 g (6¹/₂ oz) Gorgonzola cheese
4 slices Parma ham, cut in half

1 To prepare the bruschetta, cut the bread into thin slices and grill or toast to golden brown. Rub one side of each slice with the cut surface of the garlic. Drizzle with the olive oil and sprinkle with salt and freshly ground black pepper.

2 Drain the sun-dried tomato, scrape off any seeds and cut into thin strips. Press or spread the cheese onto the bruschetta, lay the Parma ham on top and garnish with strips of tomato. Season with a few twists of freshly ground black pepper and serve.

Chef's tips If Gorgonzola is too strong for your taste, use the creamier, milder Dolcelatte instead.

As a variation, marinate diced fresh tomatoes, garlic, and chopped fresh basil leaves in enough balsamic vinegar to moisten well. Drain the excess juice and place a spoonful on top of the warm slice of bruschetta.

Tomato and balsamic vinegar salad

*The syrupy balsamic vinegar used in this salad is made in the Modena area
and gives a delicious, rich bitter-sweet flavour to the dressing.*

*Preparation time **15 minutes***
*Total cooking time **Nil***
Serves 6–8

1 clove garlic, finely chopped
3 tablespoons balsamic vinegar
125 ml (4 fl oz) extra virgin olive oil
6 ripe tomatoes
2 small French shallots, finely chopped
15 g (¹/₂ oz) fresh basil leaves, finely chopped
fresh basil leaves, to garnish

1 Place the garlic in a small bowl. Add a good pinch of salt and freshly ground black pepper. Whisk in the balsamic vinegar, then gradually whisk in the olive oil until the sauce is thick and completely combined.

2 Remove the stem ends from the tomatoes and cut the tomatoes either into thin wedges or slices. Sprinkle the bottom of a serving plate with salt and freshly ground black pepper and arrange the cut tomatoes over this. Sprinkle with the French shallots and chopped basil leaves. Drizzle the vinaigrette over the tomatoes and decorate with the whole basil leaves. Keep in the refrigerator until ready to serve.

Chef's tip If you are preparing this salad ahead of time, keep in mind that the tomatoes, in contact with the salt, will begin to release their juices. If this should happen, tilt the serving plate to let the liquid run off. Wipe the edges of the plate and drizzle a little more vinaigrette over the tomatoes before serving.

Grilled scallops with prosciutto

A simple dish combining fresh, flavoursome ingredients guaranteed to delight and impress your guests.
Be careful not to overcook the prosciutto, which would cause it to become too salty.

*Preparation time **20 minutes + 20 minutes cooling***
*Total cooking time **10 minutes***
*Serves **4 as a starter***

12 large scallops
60 g (2 oz) sugar
finely grated rind of 1/2 lemon
sprig of fresh rosemary
12 slices prosciutto
50 g (13/4 oz) black olives, pitted and chopped
2 Roma (plum) tomatoes, peeled, seeded and diced
40 g (11/4 oz) capers, drained
1 clove garlic, chopped
2 tablespoons chopped fresh chives
olive oil

1 If using scallops in their shells, remove them by sliding a knife under the white muscle and orange roe. Wash the scallops to remove any grit or sand, then pull away and discard the small, tough, shiny white muscle and the black vein, leaving the orange roe intact. Dry the scallops on paper towels.

2 Put the sugar in a small pan with 100 ml (31/4 fl oz) water and heat gently, stirring to dissolve. Add the lemon rind and rosemary, increase the heat and boil for 2 minutes. Remove from the heat and leave to cool for about 20 minutes.

3 Lay the prosciutto slices on a work surface. Brush the scallops with the lemon and rosemary syrup and place one on each piece of prosciutto. Wrap the prosciutto around the scallop and secure with string or a skewer.

4 Make a relish by mixing together the olives, diced tomato, capers, garlic and 1 tablespoon of the chives. Pour in enough olive oil to bind the mixture together.

5 Brush the wrapped scallops with the olive oil and either quickly brown under a preheated hot grill or pan-fry in a non-stick pan for 1–2 minutes each side. Remove the string or skewer, then serve the scallops with a little relish beside them.

Chef's tip This recipe is also wonderful with monkfish. You will need a 1 kg (2 lb) piece of monkfish (ask your fishmonger to skin and fillet it). Use the same method as for the scallops, brushing the monkfish with syrup and wrapping the whole fish in prosciutto. Quickly brown under the grill or in a non-stick frying pan, then cook in a moderately hot 200°C (400°F/Gas 6) oven for 5–8 minutes. Cover loosely with foil and leave to rest for 5 minutes before slicing.

Mushroom ravioli in rosemary garlic cream

*Ideal as a first course or for a light lunch, the creamy sauce in this dish
truly complements the ravioli with its tasty mushroom filling.*

Preparation time 1 hour + 20 minutes cooling
Total cooking time 45 minutes
Serves 4 as a starter

PASTA
100 g (3¹/4 oz) plain flour
pinch of salt
1 teaspoon oil
1 egg, lightly beaten

MUSHROOM FILLING
olive oil, for cooking
2 French shallots, finely chopped
150 g (5 oz) button or wild mushrooms, chopped
2 tablespoons fresh breadcrumbs
*10 g (¹/4 oz) each of chopped fresh chervil, thyme,
   flat-leaf parsley and basil*

500 ml (16 fl oz) chicken stock
8 cloves garlic, roughly chopped
large sprig of fresh rosemary, cut into pieces
500 ml (16 fl oz) thick (double) cream

beaten egg, to glaze
Parmesan shavings, to garnish

1 To make the pasta, follow the method in the Chef's techniques on page 62, dividing the dough into two pieces before passing through the pasta machine.
2 To make the filling, heat a little oil over low heat and cook the shallots for 3 minutes. Add the mushrooms and a good pinch of salt. Cook, stirring, for 10 minutes, or until the mushrooms are dry. Season, to taste, then mix in the breadcrumbs, herbs and enough olive oil to just bind the mixture. Set aside.
3 To make the sauce, cook the stock and garlic over high heat for 20 minutes, or until syrupy. Remove from the heat, add the rosemary and leave to cool for about 20 minutes. Remove the rosemary, transfer the sauce to a blender or food processor and blend until smooth. Strain into a small pan, add the cream and simmer for 5 minutes, or until thick enough to coat the back of a spoon. Season and keep warm.
4 Mark one strip of the pasta dough with a round 4 cm (1¹/2 inch) pastry cutter. Place a little filling in the centre of each mark. Lightly brush around the filling with beaten egg. Place the second sheet of dough over the first sheet. Squeeze any air from between the ravioli and use the pastry cutter to cut and seal the dough.
5 Bring a large pan of salted water to the boil. Cook the ravioli for 2–3 minutes, or until *al dente*. Strain and serve with the sauce and shavings of Parmesan.

Seafood risotto

*Despite being a rather time-consuming dish to make, the final combination
of fresh seafood with creamy risotto rice is well worth the effort.*

Preparation time **55 minutes**
Total cooking time **1 hour 20 minutes**
Serves 8

500 g (1 lb) mussels
250 g (8 oz) shelled scallops
500 g (1 lb) raw prawns
750 ml (24 fl oz) white wine
1 onion, roughly chopped
1 bay leaf
2 sprigs of fresh thyme
olive oil, for cooking
4 French shallots, roughly chopped
1 celery stick, roughly chopped
1 small carrot, roughly chopped
8 cloves garlic, roughly chopped
1 onion, finely chopped
440 g (14 oz) arborio rice
125 ml (4 fl oz) thick (double) cream
60 g (2 oz) Parmesan, grated
2 tablespoons chopped fresh parsley
Parmesan shavings, to garnish

1 Scrub the mussels, remove the beards and discard any open mussels. Wash the scallops to remove any grit or sand, then pull away the small, tough, shiny white muscle and the black vein, leaving the orange roe intact. Dry the scallops on paper towels and set aside. Peel and devein the prawns, keeping the heads and shells.

2 Put the mussels, 500 ml (16 fl oz) of the wine, the roughly chopped onion, bay leaf and thyme in a large pan, cover and bring to the boil. Cook for 5 minutes, or until the mussels have opened. Remove the mussels and set aside to cool, discarding any that haven't opened.

Strain the cooking liquid through a fine sieve lined with a damp tea towel.

3 Heat about 4 tablespoons of the olive oil in a large pan and cook the peeled prawns over high heat for 2 minutes, or until pink. Remove with a slotted spoon and set aside. Add the scallops and cook for 2 minutes, then drain and set aside. Add the prawn heads and shells and cook for 2–3 minutes, or until pink, crushing with a large spoon or potato masher. Add the French shallots, celery, carrot and half the garlic and cook for 2 minutes. Add the cooking liquid from the mussels and boil for 15 minutes. Add 500 ml (16 fl oz) water, bring to the boil and cook for 10 minutes. Strain the liquid, pressing the solids to extract as much flavour as possible. Add enough water to the liquid to make up 1.75 litres and return to the pan. Bring to the boil, then reduce the heat and maintain the stock at a very low simmer.

4 Heat about 4 tablespoons of the oil over medium-low heat in a large heavy-based pan and cook the finely chopped onion for 3–5 minutes, or until soft and translucent. Add the rice and remaining garlic and stir well with a wooden spoon, making sure that the rice is completely coated with oil. Cook for 2 minutes, then add the rest of the wine, stirring well. Cook over low heat, stirring continuously, until the wine has been absorbed. Add 250 ml (8 fl oz) of the hot stock, stirring frequently until the liquid has been almost completely absorbed before adding another 250 ml (8 fl oz). Continue for 30–35 minutes, or until all the stock has been added and the rice is tender, stirring constantly to keep the rice from sticking to the bottom. Mix in the cream and Parmesan, adjust the seasoning and remove from the heat. Stir in the prawns, scallops, mussels and the chopped parsley and serve with the Parmesan shavings and some lemon wedges on the side.

Tagliatelle with wild mushrooms and leeks

While freshly made pasta will give the best results in this recipe, dried pasta could be substituted if time is short. If buying dried pasta, try to choose a good-quality pasta made from durum wheat flour only.

Preparation time **45 minutes**
Total cooking time **15 minutes**
Serves 4

PASTA
300 g (10 oz) plain flour
1 teaspoon salt
30 ml (1 fl oz) olive oil
3 eggs, lightly beaten

60 g (2 oz) unsalted butter
200 g (6¹/2 oz) wild mushrooms, such as ceps,
   slippery Jacks, Swiss browns, sliced
3 French shallots, chopped
juice of ¹/2 lemon
20 g (³/4 oz) fresh parsley, chopped
2 tablespoons sherry
8 baby leeks or 2 medium leeks, sliced
200 g (6¹/2 oz) unsalted butter, chilled and cut
   into cubes

1 To make the pasta, follow the method in the Chef's techniques on page 62, dividing the dough into four pieces before passing through the pasta machine. When the pasta has passed through the thinnest setting on the machine, pass the sheets of dough through the 6 mm (¹/4 inch) cutters to make tagliatelle.

2 Heat the butter in a frying pan, add the mushrooms and cook until starting to colour. Toss in the shallots and cook for 2–3 minutes. Add the lemon juice, parsley and sherry. Season, set aside and keep warm. Cook the leeks in boiling salted water for 2 minutes, then drain.

3 Half fill a small pan with water, bring to the boil, then remove from the heat. Place a heatproof bowl over the pan and pour in 100 ml (3¹/4 fl oz) boiling water. Whisk in the cubes of butter, piece by piece. Remove the bowl and whisk the sauce for 1 minute. Season to taste, add the leeks, cover and keep warm.

4 Cook the pasta in boiling salted water for 2 minutes, or until *al dente*. Drain, pile high on individual plates, top with the mushrooms and spoon the leek and butter sauce around.

Chef's tip If cutting the pasta by hand, after kneading and refrigerating, divide the dough into four, roll each piece into a rectangle or circle as thinly as possible and cut into strips using a sharp knife. Lay in a single layer on a lightly floured tea towel hanging over the back of a chair until ready to use.

Veal parmigiana

This dish from northern Italy successfully combines the delicacy of veal with the strong, tangy flavour of Parmesan.

Preparation time **45 minutes**
Total cooking time **1 hour 40 minutes**
Serves 4

1 kg (2 lb) large ripe tomatoes
15 g (¹/₂ oz) fresh basil
1 bay leaf
2 sprigs of fresh thyme
olive oil, for cooking
1 onion, finely chopped
3 cloves garlic, finely chopped
4 veal escalopes, about 120 g (4 oz) each
plain flour, seasoned with salt and pepper, for coating
2 eggs, lightly beaten
155 g (5 oz) fresh breadcrumbs
30 g (1 oz) Parmesan, grated
1 tablespoon finely chopped fresh parsley
120 g (4 oz) unsalted butter
250 g (8 oz) mozzarella cheese, sliced

1 Score a cross in the base of each tomato. Place in a bowl of boiling water for 10 seconds, then plunge into cold water and peel the skin away from the cross. Cut the tomatoes in half horizontally and remove the seeds with the handle of a small spoon. Chop coarsely.

2 Pull the basil leaves from their stems. Tie the stems with the bay leaf and thyme to make a bouquet garni. Heat 4 tablespoons of the olive oil in a pan and slowly cook the onion for 5 minutes without colouring. Add the tomato, garlic and bouquet garni. Season and simmer, covered, for 20 minutes, then uncovered for 45 minutes. Remove the bouquet garni and adjust the seasoning to taste.

3 Pound the veal with a meat mallet until 2 mm (¹/₈ inch) thick. Coat in the flour, patting off the excess. Toss the coated veal in the beaten egg.

4 Mix together the breadcrumbs, Parmesan and parsley in a shallow dish. Drain any excess egg from the veal and then coat with the breadcrumb mixture, pressing well with your fingers to make it stick.

5 Preheat the oven to moderately hot 200°C (400°F/Gas 6). Heat about 125 ml (4 fl oz) of the oil in a large non-stick frying pan. Add half the butter and, when it is foaming, cook two pieces of veal for about 3 minutes, or until golden brown, turning once. Drain on paper towels. Discard any leftover oil and butter from the pan and cook the remaining veal in fresh oil and butter. Arrange the veal in an ovenproof dish, cover with the mozzarella and bake for 10 minutes, or until the cheese has melted. Serve with the tomato sauce on top, garnished with the fresh basil leaves.

Cannelloni with spinach

These pasta tubes may be stuffed with a variety of fillings, whether meat, cheese or vegetable. In this recipe they are filled with spinach, coated with a creamy white sauce and baked in the oven until golden brown.

*Preparation time **1 hour + 20 minutes refrigeration***
*Total cooking time **55 minutes***
*Serves **8–10 (see Chef's tips)***

PASTA
200 g (6 1/2 oz) plain flour
1/2 teaspoon salt
20 ml (3/4 oz) olive oil
2 eggs, lightly beaten

I small onion, studded with a clove
I litre milk
I bay leaf
90 g (3 oz) unsalted butter
50 g (1 3/4 oz) plain flour
I teaspoon English mustard powder
I clove garlic, finely chopped
I kg (2 lb) English spinach, roughly chopped
pinch of grated nutmeg
2 egg yolks
30 g (1 oz) Parmesan, grated
30 g (1 oz) fresh breadcrumbs

1 To make the pasta, follow the method in the Chef's techniques on page 62, dividing the dough into two pieces before passing through the pasta machine. Roll the dough out thinly on a lightly floured surface and cut into sixteen 10 x 8 cm (4 x 3 inch) pieces. Soften in boiling salted water, a few at a time, for 1 minute. Remove with a slotted spoon and refresh in cold water to stop the cooking process. Lay the sheets on a tea towel to drain.

2 Put the onion in a pan with the milk and bay leaf. Bring slowly almost to boiling point, then remove from the heat, strain and set aside. Melt 50 g (1 3/4 oz) of the butter in a pan, remove from the heat and stir in the flour. Cook over low heat for 1–2 minutes, remove from the heat, stir in the mustard and season. Whisk in the hot milk gradually until smooth. Return to the heat and simmer, stirring, for 10 minutes, or until thick enough to coat the back of a spoon. Remove from the heat. Press buttered greaseproof paper onto the surface to prevent a skin forming, cover and set aside. Preheat the oven to moderately hot 190°C (375°F/Gas 5).

3 Melt the remaining butter over low heat and cook the garlic until softened but not coloured. Add the spinach, cover and cook over medium heat until just wilting. Season with salt, pepper and the nutmeg. Drain, return to the pan and stir in the yolks, half the Parmesan and enough of the white sauce to bind it together.

4 Lay the pasta on a board. Spoon the filling along the centre of each piece and roll up. Place in a buttered, ovenproof dish and coat with the rest of the sauce. Sprinkle with the remaining Parmesan mixed with the breadcrumbs. Bake for 20–25 minutes, or until golden.

Chef's tips It is difficult to make a smaller quantity of pasta. This recipe serves 8–10 people, so why not make it in two smaller dishes and freeze one for another time.

Instead of the fresh pasta, you could use 15–20 dried cannelloni tubes.

Osso buco

A speciality of Milan, this dish is best made using shank from the hind leg. The pieces should be cut no thicker than suggested, to ensure tenderness. Savour the bone marrow, supposedly the best part of this dish.

Preparation time **45 minutes**
Total cooking time **2 hours 30 minutes**
Serves 4

**4 veal shanks, cut into 4 cm (1¹/₂ inch) pieces
    (osso buco)**
plain flour, seasoned with salt and pepper
oil, for cooking
40 g (1¹/₄ oz) unsalted butter
1 carrot, sliced
1 celery stick, sliced
1 onion, sliced
4 cloves garlic, chopped
8 tomatoes, peeled, seeded and chopped
250 ml (8 fl oz) white wine
bouquet garni
1 litre beef stock or water
2 tablespoons chopped fresh parsley
rind of ¹/₄ orange, finely chopped
rind of ¹/₄ lemon, finely chopped

1 Preheat the oven to moderate 180°C (350°F/Gas 4). Trim the meat of any sinew or skin and lightly coat with the seasoned flour. Heat a little oil in a small non-stick frying pan and brown the veal on both sides, in batches if necessary. Set aside.

2 Melt the butter in a flameproof casserole dish and cook the carrot, celery and onion over medium heat for 3 minutes. Add the garlic and mix well, then add the chopped tomatoes and cook for 5 minutes. Add the white wine and bouquet garni and cook for another 5 minutes. Add the stock and the browned meat, bring to a simmer, season, cover and place in the oven for 1¹/₂ hours, or until the meat is tender.

3 Transfer the meat to a serving platter, cover and keep warm. Heat the cooking liquid and vegetables and bring to the boil. Skim off any fat or foam that rises to the top and cook for 20–25 minutes, or until the sauce has thickened and coats the back of a spoon. Stir in the parsley, orange and lemon rind and season to taste. Simmer for another 5 minutes, then pour over the meat and serve immediately.

Chef's tip If you prefer a milder citrus flavour, blanch the rind before using. Place it in a small pan and cover with cold water, bring to the boil for 30 seconds, then strain and refresh. Use as instructed in the recipe.

Pasta with prosciutto and Parmesan

This simple pasta dish makes the most of two of Italy's most famous ingredients—prosciutto, a salt-cured ham, and the rich, grainy Parmesan. As both of these ingredients are salty, particular care should be taken when seasoning this dish.

*Preparation time **20 minutes***
*Total cooking time **20 minutes***
Serves 4

3 tablespoons olive oil
400 g (12³/4 oz) farfalle (pasta bows)
I large onion, thinly sliced
200 g (6¹/2 oz) button mushrooms, thinly sliced
3 zucchini (courgettes), cut into batons
I large clove garlic, chopped
150 g (5 oz) prosciutto, cut into strips
300 ml (10 fl oz) crème fraîche
100 g (3¹/4 oz) Parmesan, grated
fresh basil leaves, to garnish

1 Bring a large pan two-thirds full of water to the boil. Add a good pinch of salt and 1 tablespoon of the olive oil. Add the farfalle to the bubbling water, stir with a fork and cook according to the manufacturer's instructions until the pasta is *al dente*. Pour immediately into a colander, then refresh under plenty of cold running water. Leave to drain until needed.

2 Heat a pan over high heat and add the rest of the olive oil. When the oil is hot, add the onion, mushrooms, zucchini and garlic and fry for about 2 minutes, or until the vegetables are lightly coloured. Reduce the heat, add the prosciutto strips and fry for 2–3 minutes. Stir in the crème fraîche and heat the mixture for another 2 minutes. Stir in the grated Parmesan and season to taste with salt and freshly ground black pepper.

3 Add the pasta to the pan, stir to combine and cook briefly to ensure the pasta is heated through. Serve immediately with the fresh basil leaves sprinkled over the pasta.

Veal with lemon and capers

The capers and lemon provide a sharp contrast to the buttery sauce in this classic Italian dish.

Preparation time **20 minutes**
Total cooking time **25 minutes**
Serves 4

4 veal escalopes, about 125 g (4 oz) each
plain flour, seasoned with salt and pepper
2 eggs, beaten
2 tablespoons oil
40 g (1 1/4 oz) unsalted butter
250 ml (8 fl oz) white wine
3 tablespoons capers, rinsed and drained
250 ml (8 fl oz) chicken or veal stock
1–2 tablespoons lemon juice
125 g (4 oz) unsalted butter, chilled and cubed

1 Pound the meat with a mallet until it is 3 mm (1/8 inch) thick, then cut into thirds and coat with the seasoned flour. Put the beaten egg in a bowl and mix together with 2 tablespoons water. Toss the veal in the egg mixture, shaking off any excess.

2 Heat the oil and butter in a non-stick frying pan. Cook the veal, in batches, for 3–5 minutes, until golden brown on both sides. Drain on paper towels, cover and keep warm while cooking the other veal slices.

3 Pour off the oil from the pan, add the wine and capers and cook for 8 minutes, or until almost dry. Add the stock and cook for 5 minutes, or until reduced by half. Add 1 tablespoon lemon juice, then transfer the sauce to a small pan (keeping the frying pan on one side). Whisk in the cubes of butter, without allowing the sauce to boil. Adjust the seasoning, adding more lemon juice if necessary. Transfer the veal to the frying pan, pour over the sauce, cover and leave for 2 minutes before serving.

Venetian-style liver

Tender calf's liver, rich in iron, protein and vitamin A, has a mild flavour that is perfectly enhanced by the soft caramelized onions in this Venetian recipe.

*Preparation time **20 minutes***
*Total cooking time **30 minutes***
Serves 4

500 g (1 lb) calf's liver
vegetable oil, for cooking
250 g (8 oz) onion, thinly sliced

1 Make sure the liver is completely free of veins and remove any of the thin skin that may still be attached. Slice the liver into thin strips.
2 Heat 2–3 tablespoons of the oil in a large non-stick frying pan and add the onion and a large pinch of salt. Cook over medium heat for 20–30 minutes, or until the onion is completely soft and golden brown. Remove the onion with a slotted spoon, leaving the oil in the pan.

3 Add a little more oil to the pan if necessary and heat until lightly smoking. Fry the liver in small batches, just enough to cover the base of the pan, for 1 minute, or until it has changed colour from pink to brown. Toss and cook for a moment more. Transfer each batch to a warm plate and season with salt and black pepper.
4 Return all the liver to the pan, add the cooked onion and toss to combine, but not to cook further. Transfer to a warm serving plate and serve immediately with steamed English spinach and a simple risotto.

Chef's tip The liver must fry very quickly to retain its succulence, therefore it is very important that the pan is hot or the liver will stick and fry for too long. Don't try to rush by cooking the liver in large batches—too much meat will overcrowd the pan, making the temperature drop and the liver stew rather than fry.

Rabbit and marjoram cobbler with herb scones

Italians are very fond of game, and rabbit, with its light and tender flesh, is definitely a favourite. Here it is teamed with fresh herbs, both in the stew and in the scones placed on top to soak up the flavoursome juices.

Preparation time **40 minutes**
Total cooking time **1 hour 30 minutes**
Serves 4

I rabbit, weighing 1.25 kg (2 lb 8 oz),
   cut into 8 pieces
plain flour, seasoned with salt and pepper
butter or oil, for cooking
I onion, finely chopped
150 g (5 oz) button mushrooms, sliced
I teaspoon tomato paste
I clove garlic, chopped
500 ml (16 fl oz) chicken stock
8 ripe tomatoes, peeled, seeded and chopped
I tablespoon chopped fresh rosemary
2 tablespoons chopped fresh marjoram
I tablespoon chopped fresh parsley

HERB SCONES
250 g (8 oz) self-raising flour
60 g (2 oz) unsalted butter, chilled and cut into cubes
I tablespoon chopped fresh herbs, such as parsley,
   rosemary, thyme or marjoram
120 ml (4 fl oz) buttermilk
I egg, beaten

1 Coat the rabbit in the flour. Heat a little butter or oil in a frying pan, brown the rabbit on all sides, then remove from the pan and drain on paper towels. Add the onion to the pan and cook over low heat until soft. Add the mushrooms, increase the heat and stir in the tomato paste and garlic. Transfer to a flameproof casserole, add the rabbit and season.

2 Pour in the stock (it should be enough to barely cover the rabbit) and simmer gently on the stove top for 30 minutes. Add the tomatoes and cook for a further 10 minutes. Add the rosemary, marjoram and parsley. Check that the meat is tender and season, to taste.

3 To make the scones, preheat the oven to moderately hot 200°C (400°F/Gas 6). Sift the flour and a good pinch of salt into a large bowl, add the butter and rub in until crumbly. Toss in the herbs, then stir in the milk with a knife until the dry flour has disappeared and the mixture is in large lumps. Turn out onto a lightly floured surface and gather together into a smooth ball. Roll or pat out to a 1.5 cm (5/8 inch) thickness. Work quickly—you want the dough to rise in the oven, not waste its rising power while it's being rolled. Cut into about 4 cm (1 1/2 inch) rounds, brush the tops with the egg and arrange immediately over the rabbit casserole. Place the dish near the top of the oven and bake for 12 minutes, or until the scones are golden.

Classic lasagne

*Although you can make this very popular classic Italian dish with shop-bought lasagne sheets,
the flavour and texture of thinly rolled fresh pasta is quite unique and well worth the effort.*

*Preparation time **1 hour + 20 minutes resting***
*Total cooking time **2 hours 15 minutes***
Serves 10–12

olive oil, for cooking

1 kg (2 lb) beef mince

1 large onion, finely chopped

8 cloves garlic, finely chopped

4 x 425 g (13¹/2 oz) cans peeled Italian tomatoes,
undrained and puréed in a food mill or processor

125 ml (4 fl oz) red wine

3 tablespoons tomato paste

4 sprigs of fresh thyme

1 bay leaf

650 g (1 lb 5 oz) ricotta cheese

100 ml (3¹/4 fl oz) thick (double) cream

4 eggs

400 g (12³/4 oz) mozzarella cheese, thinly sliced

50 g (1³/4 oz) Parmesan, freshly grated

PASTA
400 g (12³/4 oz) plain flour

1 teaspoon salt

2 tablespoons olive oil

4 eggs

1 Heat 2 tablespoons of the oil in a large pan until very hot. Add the beef mince and brown for 10 minutes, or until the liquid has almost evaporated. Strain off the fat and set the meat aside. Reduce the heat to low, heat a little more oil and cook the onion for 5 minutes, without colouring. Add the garlic, tomatoes, wine, tomato paste, thyme, bay leaf and beef and simmer for 45 minutes to 1 hour, or until the liquid has reduced by half.

2 To make the pasta, follow the method in the Chef's techniques on page 62, dividing the dough into four pieces before passing through the pasta machine. Drain the ricotta in a sieve, then mix with the cream and eggs in a large bowl. Season, cover and set aside. Preheat the oven to moderately hot 190°C (375°F/Gas 5).

3 Roll out the pasta dough to about 1–2 mm (¹/16 to ¹/8 inch) thick and cut into 10 x 12 cm (4 x 5 inch) rectangles. Blanch two or three sheets at a time briefly in boiling salted water, then drain on tea towels.

4 Spread about 200 ml (6¹/2 fl oz) of the meat sauce in a 3.5 litre ovenproof dish. Arrange a layer of pasta on top and cover with a third of the cheese mixture, then another layer of meat sauce. Repeat the layers twice more and finish with a layer of pasta covered with meat sauce. Cover with mozzarella and sprinkle with Parmesan. Bake for 45 minutes, or until golden brown. Leave to rest for 20 minutes before cutting.

Chicken cacciatore

Literally meaning 'hunter-style' chicken, this ever popular dish combines the flavours of mushrooms, capsicums and onions with herbs in a rich tomato sauce.

Preparation time **30 minutes**
Total cooking time **1 hour**
Serves 4

3 tablespoons olive oil
1 chicken, weighing 1.8 kg (3 lb 10 oz),
   cut into 8 pieces
2 medium onions, thinly sliced into rings
1 clove garlic, finely chopped
100 g (3¹/4 oz) button mushrooms,
   thinly sliced
1 small green capsicum (pepper), thinly sliced
3 tablespoons tomato paste
185 ml (6 fl oz) dry white wine
400 g (12³/4 oz) canned Italian tomatoes
¹/2 teaspoon dried rosemary
¹/2 teaspoon dried oregano

1 Heat the olive oil in a large frying pan. Season the chicken with salt and pepper, then fry, skin-side-down, for 5 minutes, or until lightly browned. Turn over and brown the other side. Remove and set aside.

2 Add the onion to the pan and cook for 5 minutes, then add the garlic, mushrooms and capsicum. Cook for a further 3–4 minutes, or until the onions are golden. Mix in the tomato paste and cook for 1–2 minutes, then add the wine. Bring to the boil, stirring constantly, then add the tomatoes, breaking them down with a wooden spoon. Sprinkle in the rosemary and oregano and return the chicken to the pan. Season with salt and pepper, cover and simmer for 20 minutes, stirring occasionally.

3 Check the chicken to see if it is tender—if not, cover and cook for a further 10 minutes—then transfer to a serving plate. If the sauce appears too liquid, allow to boil, uncovered, for 5 minutes. Season, to taste, then pour over the chicken. Serve immediately.

Mediterranean vegetables with polenta cakes

Polenta features strongly in the diet of northern Italy. Traditionally cut into slices with string once cooled and set, here it is fried in melted butter and served with a delicious, soft mixture of Mediterranean vegetables.

*Preparation time **35 minutes + chilling***
*Total cooking time **1 hour***
*Serves **6***

560 ml (18 fl oz) milk
210 g (7 oz) instant polenta
35 g (1¼ oz) unsalted butter
35 g (1¼ oz) Parmesan, grated
1 small red capsicum (pepper), halved and seeded
1 small green capsicum (pepper), halved and seeded
1 small yellow capsicum (pepper), halved and seeded
olive oil and butter, for cooking
1 small zucchini (courgette), cubed
1 small eggplant (aubergine), cubed
1 small red onion, cubed
120 g (4 oz) sun-dried tomatoes, cubed
4 cloves garlic, crushed
30 g (1 oz) canned chopped tomatoes, sieved

MINT AND PISTACHIO DRESSING
60 ml (2 fl oz) milk
25 g (¾ oz) shelled and skinned pistachios
30 g (1 oz) fresh mint leaves
50 ml (1¾ fl oz) pistachio or olive oil
1 clove garlic, chopped

1 Bring the milk to boiling point in a deep-sided pan and whisk in the polenta. Lower the heat and cook gently, stirring occasionally, for 5 minutes, or until smooth. Stir in the butter, Parmesan and salt and pepper, to taste. Turn out onto a greased tray and spread out to a 1.5 cm (5/8 inch) thickness. Leave to cool, then chill until set.

2 Brush the skin of the capsicums with a little oil and place, skin-side-up, under a hot grill until blackened. Put in a plastic bag or cover with a tea towel for 5 minutes, then peel away the skin. Cut the flesh into cubes.

3 To make the dressing, bring the milk to boiling point. Remove from the heat and transfer to a food processor with the pistachios, mint, oil and garlic. Lightly process, leaving small pieces of nut and mint in the mixture.

4 Heat a little olive oil in a large frying pan, add the vegetables, sun-dried tomato and garlic and toss over the heat for 8 minutes, or until tender. Add a little dressing to moisten, and 20 g (3/4 oz) of the sieved tomatoes. Season and keep warm.

5 Cut the polenta into 8 cm (3 inch) rounds with a pastry cutter or cup, then fry in a little melted butter until golden brown on both sides. Serve the polenta cakes topped with the vegetables and some mint and pistachio dressing. Arrange the remaining dressing and sieved tomato around and garnish with a few extra mint leaves to serve.

Sicilian cheesecake

This baked ricotta cheesecake with its light sponge base, citrus filling and a hint of spice is the perfect dessert to end any traditional Italian meal.

*Preparation time **30 minutes + 15 minutes cooling***
*Total cooking time **1 hour 35 minutes***
Serves 10

SPONGE
3 eggs
90 g (3 oz) caster sugar
90 g (3 oz) plain flour
15 g (1/2 oz) unsalted butter, melted, but cooled

600 ml (20 fl oz) milk
100 g (31/4 oz) vermicelli, crushed
100 g (31/4 oz) caster sugar
6 eggs, separated
410 g (13 oz) ricotta cheese
large pinch of ground cinnamon
finely grated rind of 1 lemon
60 ml (2 fl oz) orange flower water
125 g (4 oz) mixed peel, finely chopped
rind of 1 lemon, cut into fine strips
30 g (1 oz) icing sugar, to garnish

1 Preheat the oven to moderately hot 190°C (375°F/Gas 5). Grease the sides of a 23 cm (9 inch) cake or springform tin and line the base. To make the sponge, follow the method for preparing enriched sponge in the Chef's techniques on page 63, then pour the mixture into the cake tin.

2 Bake for 20 minutes, or until the centre of the sponge just springs back at the light touch of a finger. Turn out onto a wire rack to cool. Trim a layer from the top and bottom of the sponge and discard, or save for making trifle. Return the sponge to the tin.

3 Put the milk in a pan, bring just to the boil and add the vermicelli, a pinch of salt and 25 g (3/4 oz) of the caster sugar. Simmer for 25 minutes, or until the milk has been completely absorbed. Remove from the heat, leave to cool for about 15 minutes, then stir in the egg yolks. Lightly beat the ricotta in a bowl with the cinnamon, grated lemon rind, orange flower water, mixed peel and 50 g (13/4 oz) of the caster sugar. Add the vermicelli mixture.

4 Whisk the egg whites until firm peaks form. Add the remaining caster sugar and whisk until stiff and shiny. Fold into the ricotta mixture and pour over the sponge. Sprinkle with the lemon strips and bake for 45 minutes, or until firm. Leave in the tin for 5 minutes before turning out onto a wire rack to cool (the sponge layer will be on top). Dust with sifted icing sugar to serve.

Zuccotto

*A crisp coating of chocolate hides a liqueur-soaked sponge and a double layer of
cream and chocolate filling with cherries and nuts. Reminiscent of the wonderful ice-cream cakes
of Italy, which surprise you with the different flavours of each melting mouthful.*

*Preparation time **45 minutes + chilling***
*Total cooking time **30 minutes***
*Serves **8***

SPONGE
3 eggs
125 g (4 oz) caster sugar
100 g (3 1/4 oz) plain flour
25 g (3/4 oz) cocoa powder
25 g (3/4 oz) unsalted butter, melted, but cooled

30 ml (1 fl oz) maraschino liqueur or Kirsch
30 ml (1 fl oz) brandy
300 ml (10 fl oz) thick (double) cream
50 g (1 3/4 oz) icing sugar
***50 g (1 3/4 oz) almonds, toasted and finely chopped
(see Chef's tips)***
***50 g (1 3/4 oz) hazelnuts, toasted and chopped (see
Chef's tips)***
40 g (1 1/4 oz) good-quality dark chocolate, chopped
50 g (1 3/4 oz) glacé cherries, chopped
***330 g (10 1/2 oz) good-quality dark chocolate, melted
(see Chef's tips)***
25 g (3/4 oz) white chocolate

1 Preheat the oven to moderate 180°C (350°F/Gas 4).
Line a 1-litre capacity bowl with plastic wrap (if you
have one, use a bowl with a completely round base).
Grease a 25 cm (10 inch) square and a 15 cm (6 inch)
square cake tin and line both with baking paper.

2 To make the sponge, follow the method for preparing
enriched sponge in the Chef's techniques on page 63,
then pour the mixture into the two cake tins and bake
for 10 minutes, or until firm to the touch. Cool on a
wire rack and peel off the baking paper.

3 Using a flan ring, plate or cake tin as a guide, cut a
25 cm (10 inch) circle from the larger sponge. Cut out
a small wedge (like cutting a slice of cake) to make it
more pliable and easier to fit into the round bowl. Push
the sponge gently into the bowl to line it, cutting off any
that overlaps. From the second sponge, cut a circle the
same size as the bowl top. Brush all the sponge with the
combined liqueur and brandy.

4 To prepare the filling, whisk the cream and icing
sugar to soft peaks and divide into two bowls. To the
first bowl, add the nuts, chopped chocolate and cherries.
Spoon into the sponge-lined bowl and hollow out the
centre with the back of a spoon, making sure the layer
of cream is even. Refrigerate for 30 minutes to set.

5 Mix a third of the melted chocolate into the second
bowl of whipped cream—mixing with a little of the
cream first, before adding to the rest. Spoon into the
hollowed centre of the chilled Zuccotto, level using a
palette knife and press the circle of sponge on top.
Refrigerate for 30 minutes.

6 Invert the bowl onto a wire rack and turn out the
Zuccotto. Take the remaining melted dark chocolate and
stir to cool slightly. Pour over the Zuccotto and tap the
rack to make sure the chocolate covers the whole of the
sponge. Refrigerate until set. Melt the white chocolate
and flick it over the Zuccotto with a fork. Chill to set
before serving.

Chef's tips To roast the hazelnuts and almonds, place on
a baking tray and roast in the oven at moderate 180°C
(350°F/Gas 4) for about 3–5 minutes, taking care not to
let the nuts burn.

To melt the chocolate, place it in a bowl over a pan
half-full of water that has come to the boil and been
removed from the heat. The steaming water will gently
warm the chocolate.

Tiramisù

Layers of sponge biscuits soaked in coffee and Kahlua, rich mascarpone cream and a generous dusting of cocoa powder have contributed to the enormous success of this dessert today.

Preparation time **35 minutes + chilling**
Total cooking time **Nil**
Serves **4–6**

3 egg yolks
120 g (4 oz) caster sugar
180 g (5³/4 oz) mascarpone
300 ml (10 fl oz) cream, for whipping
3 tablespoons Kahlua
500 ml (16 fl oz) strong coffee, cooled
36 sponge finger biscuits
cocoa powder, for dusting

1 Beat the egg yolks with the sugar until the sugar has dissolved and the mixture is light. Add the mascarpone and mix well. Beat the cream into stiff peaks and gently fold into the mascarpone mixture, then spread a thin layer of the mascarpone cream over the base of a deep 35 cm (14 inch) oval dish.

2 Add the Kahlua to the coffee. Dip the sponge fingers into the coffee, soaking them well. Depending on the freshness of the biscuits, they may require more or less soaking, but be careful not too oversoak. Arrange a layer of sponge fingers close together in the dish—you may need to break them to fit the shape of your dish. Cover with another layer of the mascarpone cream, then another layer of sponge fingers, arranging them in the opposite direction to the first layer. Repeat the layers, finishing with mascarpone cream. Smooth the top and keep chilled until ready to serve. Generously dust with cocoa powder just before serving. Tiramisù is best made several hours in advance so that the flavours have time to blend before serving.

Baked peaches with mascarpone cream

*As each sealed parcel is opened, the tantalising aroma is a
preview of the delicious flavour captured within.*

*Preparation time **20 minutes***
*Total cooking time **20 minutes***
Serves 4

20 g (³/4 oz) unsalted butter
20 g (³/4 oz) caster sugar
I egg, lightly beaten
I tablespoon plain flour
20 g (³/4 oz) ground almonds
I drop almond essence
2 fresh peaches, peeled and halved,
   or 4 tinned peach halves
10 g (¹/4 oz) flaked almonds, toasted (see Chef's tip)
30 ml (I fl oz) Cointreau, Kirsch or Grand Marnier
ground cinnamon, to dust

MASCARPONE CREAM
250 g (8 oz) mascarpone
125 ml (4 fl oz) thick (double) cream
2 teaspoons caster sugar
4 drops vanilla extract or essence
4 drops Cointreau

1 Cut out four circles of baking paper or foil, 6 cm
(2¹/2 inches) bigger all round than the peach halves.

Preheat the oven to moderate 180°C (350°F/Gas 4). To
make the almond filling, beat together the butter and
sugar until smooth. Beat in half the egg until well
incorporated and mix in the flour—the mixture should
be smooth and pale. Stir in the ground almonds and
almond essence and beat in enough of the remaining egg
to give a soft mixture that just holds its shape.

2 Place each peach half, cut-side-up, in the centre of a
circle of baking paper or foil. Put the almond filling into
a piping bag fitted with a plain nozzle and pipe a good
mound into each peach half, or spoon the mixture in
neatly, filling the space where the stone was. Sprinkle
with the flaked almonds, drizzle with the liqueur and
dust with a pinch of cinnamon.

3 Fold up the paper around the peach halves and twist
along the edges to seal. Place on a baking tray, sealed-
side-up, and bake in the oven for 15 minutes, or until
the parcels have puffed. Remove the peaches from the
parcels, or just open the sealed top, to serve.

4 To make the mascarpone cream, beat together all the
ingredients until smooth and thick. Serve with the
peach parcels.

Chef's tip To toast the almonds, place on a baking tray
and roast in a moderate oven 180°C (350°F/Gas 4) for
1–2 minutes, taking care not to let the nuts burn.

Chocolate hazelnut torte

The toasted hazelnut meringue is enhanced by a chocolate, hazelnut mousse that is lightly set and used to fill and coat the torte.

Preparation time **40 minutes + chilling**
Total cooking time **20 minutes**
Serves 8

HAZELNUT MERINGUE
2 egg whites
60 g (2 oz) caster sugar
**60 g (2 oz) lightly roasted hazelnuts, ground
   (see Chef's tip)**

HAZELNUT MOUSSE
2 leaves gelatine or 1 teaspoon gelatine powder
60 g (2 oz) caster sugar
3 eggs
1 tablespoon cocoa powder
150 g (5 oz) good-quality dark chocolate, melted
50 g (1³/4 oz) chocolate hazelnut spread
60 g (2 oz) unsalted butter, beaten until soft
200 ml (6¹/2 fl oz) cream, for whipping

60 g (2 oz) roasted hazelnuts, chopped (see Chef's tip)
cocoa powder and icing sugar, to dust

1 Preheat the oven to warm 160°C (315°F/Gas 2–3). To make the hazelnut meringue, draw three 20 cm (8 inch) circles on baking paper and place on a baking tray. Beat the egg whites to firm peaks, sprinkle with the sugar and beat until stiff. Fold in the hazelnuts. Divide the mixture among the three circles and spread with the back of a spoon. Bake for 7 minutes, or until golden brown and dry. Cool on a wire rack.

2 If you are using gelatine leaves, place in cold water to soak. Put the sugar with 30 ml (1 fl oz) water in a small pan and bring slowly to the boil. Boil for 6 minutes, or until the sugar syrup reaches 118°C (240°F) on a sugar thermometer, or a little forms a soft ball when dropped into cold water. Put the eggs in a large bowl and begin to whisk. Pour on the bubbling syrup, aiming between the whisk and the side of the bowl. Whisk continuously until a firm trail is left when the whisk is lifted away.

3 Squeeze out the gelatine leaves and melt in a bowl over steaming water. If you are using powdered gelatine, dissolve it in a little water. Pour the gelatine onto the warm egg mixture, add the cocoa, chocolate and chocolate hazelnut spread and whisk well. Add the butter and mix until smooth. Semi-whip the cream, then fold into the mixture and chill until thickened.

4 Spread a thick layer of mousse over two of the meringue discs, layer one upon the other and put the remaining meringue on top. Cover the top and the side with the remaining mousse, making peaks with a knife. Chill. Press the hazelnuts around the side and sprinkle a few on top. Dust with the cocoa, then the icing sugar.

Chef's tip To toast the hazelnuts, place on a baking tray and roast in a moderate oven 180°C (350°F/Gas 4) for 3–5 minutes, taking care not to let the nuts burn.

Zabaglione with sponge fingers

This deliciously light Zabaglione must be eaten immediately after it is made.
It takes only a few minutes to whisk and serve and is perfect for unexpected guests.

Preparation time **15 minutes**
Total cooking time **20 minutes**
Serves **4–5**

SPONGE FINGERS
2 eggs, separated
50 g (1³/4 oz) caster sugar
50 g (1³/4 oz) plain flour
icing sugar, to dust

ZABAGLIONE
4 egg yolks
100 g (3¹/4 oz) caster sugar
75 ml (2¹/2 fl oz) Marsala

1 Preheat the oven to moderately hot 200°C (400°F/ Gas 6). Line a baking tray with greaseproof paper. Fit a piping bag with a 1 cm (¹/2 inch) plain nozzle.
2 To make the sponge fingers, whisk the egg yolks and sugar in a bowl until creamy and almost white. In a separate bowl, whisk the egg whites until stiff peaks form as the whisk is lifted away. With a large metal spoon or plastic spatula, fold a third of the egg white into the yolk mixture. Sift half the flour into the yolk mixture and carefully fold in, then add another portion of egg white. Repeat with the remaining flour and egg white, taking care not to overmix. Spoon the mixture into the piping bag and pipe 8 cm (3 inch) lengths slightly apart on the baking tray. Dust liberally with the sifted icing sugar, then leave at room temperature for 5 minutes to dissolve the sugar and create a pearl effect. Bake for 10 minutes, or until golden brown. Remove the sponge fingers from the tray by lifting the greaseproof paper with the biscuits, then placing them upside-down on the work surface. Sprinkle the back of the paper with water to make it easy to peel away. Turn the biscuits over and cool on a wire rack.
3 To make the Zabaglione, bring a pan half-full of water to the boil, then turn the heat as low as possible. Whisk the egg yolks and sugar in a heatproof bowl until almost white. Mix in the Marsala. Place the bowl over the barely steaming water and whisk until the mixture increases to four times its volume and is firm and frothy. Pour into four large wine glasses and serve immediately with the sponge fingers.

Chef's tip Zabaglione is an excellent standby dessert for unexpected guests. If you do not have the traditional Italian Marsala, use Madeira instead.

Chef's techniques

◆

Making pasta

See the list of ingredients in each pasta recipe to find out the quantity of flour, salt, olive oil and eggs needed to make the pasta dough for each dish. Fresh pasta should be used on the same day it is made.

Place the flour, salt, olive oil and eggs in a food processor and mix in short bursts until the mixture forms large crumbs.

Fold the sheet into three and pass through the machine again at the thickest setting. Repeat this rolling and folding ten times, lightly flouring the pasta dough and machine to prevent sticking.

Gently press the mixture between your finger and thumb to check if it will come together smoothly. If not, continue to process for a few bursts.

Without folding, continue to pass the dough through progressively thinner settings, until it has passed through the finest setting. Repeat with the remaining portions of dough.

Turn out onto a lightly floured surface and knead for 2 minutes into a smooth dough. Wrap in plastic wrap and refrigerate for 20 minutes. Secure a pasta machine to the edge of a table.

To make tagliatelle, adjust the roller settings to cut to the width stated in the recipe. Pass each sheet of dough through the lightly floured cutters. Lay in a single layer on a floured tea towel hanging over the back of a chair.

Divide the dough into two or four pieces. Keep covered and work with one piece at a time. Flatten into a rectangle and roll through the lightly floured pasta machine on the thickest setting.

To make lasagne sheets, cut the pasta sheets to the size stated in the recipe and place side-by-side on a tea towel. Cover with another tea towel and leave until ready to use.

Preparing whole artichokes

You can cook either the whole artichoke, as shown below, or just the heart. Both are delicious.

Break off the artichoke stalk at the bottom, pulling out the fibres that attach it to the base.

Pull off the outer leaves and place the artichoke in a pan of boiling salted water with the juice of 1 lemon. Weigh down with a plate and simmer for 20–35 minutes.

Test for doneness by pulling at one of the leaves. If it comes away easily, the artichoke is done. Cut off the top half of the artichoke and discard.

Remove the hairy choke in the middle of the artichoke with a spoon. The artichoke bottom is now ready to use.

Enriched sponge

A sponge enriched with melted butter has a moist texture and can be plain or flavoured with cocoa.

Whisk the eggs and sugar in a large bowl over a pan of steaming water until the mixture is light and frothy and leaves a trail. Remove the bowl from the pan and whisk until the mixture is cold.

Fold the sifted dry ingredients (flour and, if using, cocoa powder) into the mixture with a large metal spoon, being careful not to overfold and lose volume.

Pour the cooled, melted butter down the side of the bowl and gently fold in, being careful not to lose any volume.

Published by Murdoch Books® a division of Murdoch Magazines Pty Limited, 45 Jones Street, Ultimo NSW 2007.

Murdoch Books and Le Cordon Bleu thank the 32 masterchefs of all the Le Cordon Bleu Schools, whose knowledge and expertise have made this book possible, especially: Chef Cliche (MOF), Chef Terrien, Chef Boucheret, Chef Duchêne (MOF), Chef Guillut, Chef Steneck, Paris; Chef Males, Chef Walsh, Chef Hardy, London; Chef Chantefort, Chef Bertin, Chef Jambert, Chef Honda, Tokyo; Chef Salembien, Chef Boutin, Chef Harris, Sydney; Chef Lawes, Adelaide; Chef Guiet, Chef Denis, Ottawa. Of the many students who helped the Chefs test each recipe, a special mention to graduates David Welch and Allen Wertheim. A very special acknowledgment to Directors Susan Eckstein, Great Britain, and Kathy Shaw, Paris, who have been responsible for the coordination of the Le Cordon Bleu team throughout this series.

Murdoch Books®
Managing Editor: Kay Halsey
Series Concept, Design and Art Direction: Juliet Cohen
Editor: Jane Price
Food Director: Jody Vassallo
Food Editors: Roslyn Anderson, Tracy Rutherford
Designer: Michèle Lichtenberger
Photographer: Joe Filshie
Food Stylist: Carolyn Fienberg
Food Preparation: Jo Forrest
Chef's Techniques Photographers: Reg Morrison, Tim Cole
Home Economists: Michelle Lawton, Kerrie Mullins, Justine Poole, Kerrie Ray

CEO & Publisher: Anne Wilson
Publishing Director: Catie Ziller
General Manager: Mark Smith
Creative Director: Marylouise Brammer
International Sales Director: Mark Newman

National Library of Australia Cataloguing-in-Publication Data
Italian. ISBN 0 86411 744 2. 1. Cookery, Italian. (Series: Le Cordon Bleu home collection). 641.5945

Printed by Toppan Printing (S) Pte Ltd
First Printed 1998
©Design and photography Murdoch Books® 1998
©Text Le Cordon Bleu 1998

Distributed in the UK by D Services, 6 Euston Street, Freemen's Common, Leicester LE2 7SS Tel 0116-254-7671 Fax 0116-254-4670. Distributed in Canada by Whitecap (Vancouver) Ltd, 351 Lynn Avenue, North Vancouver, BC V7J 2C4 Tel 604-980-9852 Fax 604-980-8197 or Whitecap (Ontario) Ltd, 47 Coldwater Road, North York, ON M3B 1Y8 Tel 416-444-3442 Fax 416-444-6630

The Publisher and Le Cordon Bleu wish to thank Carole Sweetnam for her help with this series.
Front cover: Veal with lemon and capers.

IMPORTANT INFORMATION

CONVERSION GUIDE

1 cup = 250 ml (8 fl oz)
1 Australian tablespoon = 20 ml (4 teaspoons)
1 UK tablespoon = 15 ml (3 teaspoons)

NOTE: We have used 20 ml tablespoons. If you are using a 15 ml tablespoon, for most recipes the difference will be negligible. For recipes using baking powder, gelatine, bicarbonate of soda and flour, add an extra teaspoon for each tablespoon specified.

CUP CONVERSIONS—DRY INGREDIENTS

1 cup flour, plain or self-raising = 125 g (4 oz)
1 cup sugar, caster = 250 g (8 oz)
1 cup breadcrumbs, dry = 125 g (4 oz)

IMPORTANT: Those who might be at risk from the effects of salmonella food poisoning (the elderly, pregnant women, young children and those suffering from immune deficiency diseases) should consult their GP with any concerns about eating raw eggs.